All Things are Possible

*"**Blessed** are they that have not seen, and yet have **believed.**"*
(John 20:29)

All Things are Possible

A Monthly faith building devotional for women

By Rebecca Johnston

All Things Are Possible
Monthly Faith Building Devotional for Women

Paraphrased scriptures do not necessarily suggest copyright holder's interpretation or intent.

ISBN: 978-0-9663917-3-2

Printed in the United States of America.

Edited by Mark F. Johnston, breakthroughvictory.com

Dedication

Thank you, God, for being my everything. For always loving me where I am and never abandoning me. To my husband Mark, thank you for being my husband, editor, and best friend for life; thank you for always believing in me when I found it hard to believe in myself. To my children, Leena and Deric, thank you for your unconditional love and patience with me as I continue to grow as a Christian mom. To my parents for their love.

To all the women who will read this book and find encouragement to be stronger in the Lord. My prayer for each one of you is that you fully understand how precious you are to God. How God loves you where you are and wants you to be the best version of yourself that He knows you can be. That you understand your worth and your purpose here on earth.

In God's love,

Rebecca

"And whatever you ask in prayer, you will receive, if you have faith." (Matthew 21:22)

Table of Contents

And Jesus said to him, "'If you can'! All things are possible for one who believes." (Mark 9:23)

Foreword

Dear reader, Though this book is about doing good things, that is not its first aim. Its first aim is to share faith-boosting scriptures (the good news!) and provide activities that will hopefully help you actualize them in accordance with the Lord's command that we not only "hear the word but be *doers* of it." The overarching goal is to help you draw closer to the Lord to know Him better.

The common denominator between many of these activities is that they seek to remove something rather than add something. This is not a coincidence. The Bible teaches that "in order for God to increase we must decrease," and that means ridding ourselves of "everything that hinders" our faith in Him. So, think of this book as an aid to help you remove a lot of extra "baggage" and weight that might be hindering your faith walk and spiritual progress in knowing the Lord.

That said, these activities are very difficult without God. But as the book title states, "All Things are Possible" with God's power and endurance. I am a witness this is 100% true. So, turn to God and ask Him for strength and endurance to conquer these activities. He will give you everything you need to be victorious in Christ.

Mark Johnston
Author, Editor, Minister
Breakthroughvictory.com

*"Now **faith** is the assurance of things hoped for, and the certainty of things not seen." (Hebrews 11:1)*

Introduction

Hello all you wonderful ladies!

I am overjoyed and beyond grateful that you have decided to put legs to your prayers and embark on a year of new faith activities that I know will draw you closer to God and improve your health and life in every way. I have no doubt this book is going to be a great blessing to you if you persevere with God's power. I am so excited for you!

Did you know the Bible says you are *precious* to God? It's true:

> *"I have called you by name, you are mine… You are precious in my eyes, and honored, and I love you." (Isaiah 43:1-4)*

If we believe this (and I hope you do!) then we must also believe that God wants the very best for us and that includes great health:

> *"Beloved, I pray that all may go well with you and that you may be in good health, as it goes well with your soul." (3 John 1:2)*

Good health goes well with our soul. God not only wants us to have good health, He wants us to live orderly, meaningful, purposeful, and holy lives that are pleasing to Him and a blessing to others. The problem is, many of us—including myself—never learned that in order to live holy lives we must develop good habits.

Developing good habits is hard because it requires virtues such as self-control, patience, and perseverance, which don't come naturally for most people. In order to possess these virtues, we need God's help because He is the *Source* of all of them (see Galatians 5:22).

When the Lord first revealed to me through His word that I had a lot of not-so-good habits (especially reliance on alcohol), I did not believe it. I didn't think having a drink or two after work every night and on the weekends was a problem. Nevertheless, I kept feeling convicted, so I turned to God and asked Him to reveal His will to me.

Then something happened. One Christmas eve I put a sparkling bottle of vodka under our tree, arranged it with the other gifts, and took a picture of it. Just as I thought to myself, "Oh that's so beautiful," my husband kidded, "You know you love alcohol when you put it under the tree and take photos of it."

Ouch! He said it with a laugh, and I laughed along with him, but deep inside I heard the voice of the Holy Spirit telling me alcohol had become more than just a social beverage to me; it had become my comfort and counselor—the two very things God was supposed to be in my life.

Realizing I was putting more faith in the bottle than God, I was moved to take a break from drinking for a while. Quitting cold turkey was out of the question, so I had the idea to quit for 30 days instead. "How hard can it be?" I kidded myself. Then I heard the Lord's voice through His word reminding me:

"Your spirit is indeed willing but your flesh is weak." (Matthew 26:40)

A few days into the activity it hit me that 30 days without a shot of *liquid hope* was going to be a lot harder than I thought. I turned to God for help to endure the trial, and He responded through His word:

"You can do all things through Christ who strengthens you" (Philippians 4:13).

I was so grateful for that liberating truth. I finally came to understand that *all things* are possible with the resurrection *power* of Jesus and started prayerfully turning to Him daily for help. He did not disappoint. Through the truth of His word He gave me amazing faith, will power, and self control.

The rest is history. After conquering the alcohol activity, I created more thirty-day activities and tackled them the same way: by reading God's word with my husband, meditating on it together, praying, and drawing strength from Christ. Consequently, my faith became stronger and so did my will to please God.

Now I am pleased to present the same activities I have faced and conquered with faith to help you too grow more dependent on God and develop good habits. I have included empowering scriptures to meditate on, as well as reading assignments, with every activity. These Scriptures are specific to the activity, so read them carefully and meditate on them. You will gain faith and conquering power, which is what you need to demolish bad habits and develop good habits.

Remember:

"All scripture is given by inspiration of God, and is profitable for doctrine, for reproof, for correction, for instruction in righteousness." (2 Timothy 3:16)

I've also added "helpers," which are ideas to get your creative juices flowing, and a blank journal (at the back of the book) for you to write down your learnings, activities, prayers, and progress.

You will need God's faith and strength for these activities. Say this daily:

"Father, your power is made perfect in my weakness." (2 Corinthians 12:9)

Don't "try to be strong." You will burn out. Instead, find your strength from God through confession and prayer. When you confess your weakness to God, He will make you strong!

"Lord Jesus, apart from you I can do nothing, but with you I can do all things." (John 15:5)

And don't be too hard on yourself. If you can't make it through an entire month, take a break, then regroup and try again the next month. Extend "grace" to yourself. If it takes more than a year to get through these activities, don't beat yourself up—but don't give up either. *Faithful perseverance* is the key to victory. It might help to do these activities with a friend or family member. We are stronger together.

As you face these new activities, I hope you will turn to the Lord and ask for faith, *self-control,* strength, and belief in His *power* to help you. I pray you will be convicted and empowered by the Spirit of Truth to endure and grow your relationship with God. I pray His peace will fill you, and you will *know* that *all things* are possible through Him. And I pray God gives you blessed assurance of victory through Christ and that your victories become great testimonies for God's glory.

Daily Surrender Prayer

Here is a daily surrender prayer to start praying every day while you are getting ready for your day:

Start by placing your palms up and asking the Lord to fill you with the spirit of truth. Then turn your palms down to show God your desire to give Him all your cares, fears, anxieties. Then pray each one out loud and ask Him to take them away. Then turn your palms up again and ask the Lord to receive His blessings of healing, courage, strength, peace, joy, and faith. Then pray "In Jesus name, amen."

"For nothing will be impossible with God." (Luke 1:37)

Activity 1: Pray for Faith

"Today is the day the Lord has made, I will rejoice and be glad." (Psalm 118:24)

"All things are possible for He who believes." (Mark 9:23)

"Faith comes by hearing the word of God." (Romans 10:17)

As you know, life is hard and filled with many obstacles. When times are rough and we can't see the light at the end of the tunnel, it's easy to start grumbling and even want to give up. Thankfully, if we confess our weakness and ask God for the *power* of faith and self-control to overcome our obstacles and activities, He will give it to us. So, in preparation for this year-long faith journey, the first activity is to learn more about faith and ask God for it.

To get started, *carefully* read the scriptures I have listed below. As you read, use the space at the end of this chapter or the journal at the end of the book to note the words or verses that speak to your heart about faith. Pay special attention to verses about *trusting God* and *drawing strength* from Him. Do not skip this faith building activity; you will need it for next month's activity! By the way, this first activity can be done in less than a month.

Scripture Reading

Read, journal, and meditate on Hebrews 11, Mark 9:14-29, and Mark 11:22 for the next two weeks to a month. They are all about faith.

Helpers

Recite these prayerful affirmations frequently with faith. You might also want to write them on little cards and place them in your purse so you have constant access to them. There is great faith-building and self-control building power in God's word!

> *"God is faithful, and he will not let me be tempted beyond my ability, If I am tempted, He will also provide a way of escape, so I can endure the trial." (1 Corinthians 10:13)*
>
> *"All things are possible for me because I believe." (Mark 9:23)*
>
> *"I can do all things through Christ who strengthens me." (Philippians 4:13)*
>
> *"If God is for me, who can be against me?" (Romans 8:31)*
>
> *"I wait for the Lord, my soul waits, and in his word I hope." (Psalm 130:5)*
>
> *"Father in heaven, I believe, help my unbelief! In Jesus name, amen." (Mark 9:24)*

Notes:

God said, "My power is made ***perfect*** *in your weakness." (2 Corinthians 12:9)*

Activity 2: Take a Break From a "Go-to" Comfort

"A person without self-control is like a city broken into and left without walls." (Proverbs 25:28)

"But I discipline my body and keep it under control." (1 Corinthians 9:12)

Remember I said in the Introduction that you would need faith for this activity? I wasn't kidding. Most of us have at least one go-to "comfort" food, drink, or other thing (like cigarettes or vaping) we "turn to" to get us through trials and times of doubt and discouragement. Comfort go-to's are so intertwined in our lives that we think they are totally normal and good. But that's not what the Bible says.

The Bible says our comfort, counsel, and courage (the "three C's") should come not from vodka, wine, lattes, or ice cream but rather from God:

"Praise be to the God and Father of our Lord Jesus Christ, the Father of compassion and the God of <u>all comfort</u>, who comforts us in all our troubles, so that we can comfort those in any trouble with the comfort we ourselves receive from God." (2 Corinthians 1:3)

"When anxiety was great within me, your comfort brought me joy." (Psalm 94:19)

"For to us a child is born, to us a son is given; and his name shall be called Wonderful Counselor, Mighty God, Everlasting Father, Prince of Peace." (Isaiah 9:6)

"Fear not, for I am with you; be not dismayed, for I am your God; I will strengthen you, I will help you, I will uphold you with my righteous right hand." (Isaiah 41:10)

Typically, most of us seek comfort and assurance the most when we are discouraged, fearful, anxious, or feeling hopeless. Comforting devices help us convince ourselves that there is hope and "everything is going to be OK." In a sense, they are faith-building medicines. But God wants us to put all our faith and hope in Him.

God, through His Holy Spirit in us, wants to be our sole comforter, counselor, and encourager. He wants us to have *blessed assurance* that things are going to be OK because He is all powerful and because all His promises (especially our salvation) are true. This is why He says:

"Cast all your anxieties on me because I care for you." (1 Peter 5:7)

So, to help you become more dependent on God's word for comfort and hope and less dependent on food and drink, this month's activity is to take a break from your go-to comfort device. I chose alcohol, but if you don't drink you can also take a break from your morning latte or whatever else you rely on to get through the day.

Scripture Reading

Each morning say the Lord's Prayer (Matthew 6:9), then read five Psalms and one Proverb. At that rate, you should be able to get through both books in a month. Starting your day off with God's word, His "daily bread," will change your outlook on the day ahead and give your mind and heart peace like nothing and no one else can. Psalms is filled with prayers to God for strength and affirmations of His power, and Proverbs is filled with wisdom for navigating this life and living in a way that is pleasing to God. Watch how your outlook improves during this activity.

Helpers

- If you choose to stop drinking, sip water all day. Stay hydrated. Have a fizzy water with a slice of lime in a fancy glass in the evening.
- Read scriptures in the morning and before you go to bed at night.
- If you are hurting, go to a quiet room by yourself and pray to the Lord for help. Pour out your heart to Him. Pray with belief, "Father, my spirit is willing but my flesh is weak. Please give me strength to please you. I know all thing are possible

through Christ who strengthens me. In Jesus name, I believe, help my unbelief, amen."

- Take a walk and listen to soothing music.
- Avoid stressful TV or other "entertainment" that provokes your flesh to anger or anxiety.
- Take a break from toxic or agitating people.

Notes:

God said, "Cast all your anxieties on me because I care for you." (1 Peter 5:7)

Activity 3: Give Daily

"But if anyone has the world's goods and sees his brother in need, yet closes his heart against him, how does God's love abide in him?" (1 John 3:17)

"Give, and it will be given to you. Good measure, pressed down, shaken together, running over, will be put into your lap. For with the measure you use it will be measured back to you." (Luke 6:38)

God says a great deal about giving in the Bible, notably, "We must help the weak, remembering the words the Lord Jesus himself said: 'It is more blessed to give than to receive.'" (Acts 20:35)

Most people usually feel great after doing something for someone else. I can't think of a time that I was charitable with my "time, talents, or treasures," and not rewarded by The Lord in some way. Now, receiving blessings should not be our motivation for being charitable (our motivation should come from our faith); our motivation should be our faith and love for God. That said, we can rest assured God will take care of us and the spirit of giving will go well with our souls.

The activity for the next 30 days is to give at least one thing every day. It might be hard, but remember, you can do all things through Christ!

Ideas for Giving

Giving comes in far more ways than just physical items and money. Here are some ideas.

- Send an encouraging scripture to someone.
- Share a genuinely felt compliment with someone.
- Share a snack or portion of your lunch with someone.
- Volunteer at a local charity.
- Clean out your garage and donate old tools or toys to a local thrift store.
- Encourage someone who has grown weary or lost heart.
- Drop some cookies or cupcakes off at your favorite local business.
- Give a coffee card to restaurant or retail employee.
- Express your thanks to a local law enforcement officer, health care worker, or first responder.

Scripture Reading

Read a little of the Apostle Paul's first letter to the Corinthians every morning. Take note of any passages that "jump out at you," and ask God to reveal their deeper meanings to you. If you reach the end before the end of the month, read his second letter to the Corinthians.

Helpers

- Post a reminder to yourself to give daily on your bathroom mirror or computer screen (wherever you will see it in the morning).
- If you are having a tough day and feel grumpy or ungiving, ask the Lord to soften your heart. Pray, "Lord, create in me a pure heart, and renew a steadfast spirit of giving and thankfulness within me. In Jesus name, amen.
- Make a list of all the things you are grateful for, and as you consider them, think about how much they would bless someone else.

Notes:

Activity 4: Take a Break From Extra Spending

"And my God will supply every need of yours according to his riches in glory in Christ Jesus." (Philippians 4:19)

We often mistake our wants for our needs and convince ourselves why we must have something. I don't know about you, but I often find myself wanting something I already have, such as clothes, makeup, and kitchen gadgets. But when I am in the word of God and have the spirit of thankfulness and contentment, I can clearly *see* I need no more than God has already provided.

For this activity, do your best to buy nothing other than food and house necessities for thirty days. When you go to add something to your shopping cart ask yourself: "Do I really need this? Or can something I already have at home suffice?"

At the grocery store, my husband and I remind each other to #ProtectTheCart! What goes in your cart goes in your body (which the Lord calls your "temple").

Scripture Reading

Read the Gospel of Matthew Chapter 6, verses 19 through 34. Journal anything that really jumps out at you. Meditate on this chapter all month and ask the Lord to help you believe it in your heart and live it.

Helpers

- To help you with this activity, take a break from shopping your favorite stores like Ross, Marshall's, Hobby Lobby, the mall, Amazon, or any other store that tempts you to buy things you don't need.
- If you feel weak and tempted: stop, breathe deep, ask God for help. Affirm His power out loud and pray, "God I know you are all powerful. Please give me the strength to resist this temptation and trust that you will provide for all my needs. In Jesus name, Amen."

Notes:

"God will supply ***every need*** *of yours according to his riches in glory in Christ Jesus." (Philippians 4:19)*

Do you believe this? If yes, declare it out loud today and tell your doubts and fears to get behind you! If no, pray to God for belief.

Activity 5: Improve Body and Mind Health

"Or do you not know that your body is a temple of the Holy Spirit within you, whom you have from God? You are not your own, for you were bought with a price. So glorify God in your body." (1 Corinthians 6:19-20)

"A joyful heart is good medicine, but a crushed spirit dries up the bones." (Proverbs 17:22)

God wants us to care for our bodies (temples). We please Him when we keep our bodies and minds free from toxic spirits and impurities. The first step to good physical and mental health is to guard our eyes, ears, and stomachs from things that aren't healthy for us (and by that, I mean things that don't draw us closer to God and equip us to better serve Him).

Exercising and eating right are non-negotiable necessities for good mind and body health, and therefore we must make them priorities. For the next 30 days, do your best to: first, consume only healthy, whole, and nutritious foods. ("whole" means no fillers, no processing, and no ingredients you can't pronounce); and second, do some form of exercise 6 days a week.

Remember that you were bought at a price and God wants you to honor your body temple by staying healthy.

Scripture Reading

Read Johns first letter (1 John) to the church and meditate on the parts about being cleansed and cleaned by Christ.

Body Helpers

- Try the "Whole30" program. (Google it)
- Protect your cart and only put good things in it.
- Walk around the block a few times every morning.
- Buy a stationary bike and ride 2 miles daily.
- Get a gym membership.
- Follow a YouTube at-home workout or yoga program.

Mind Helpers

- Read the Bible for 5 minutes in the morning and 5 minutes in the evening.
- Don't watch 'dark' shows or movies.
- Avoid negative and toxic people.
- Listen to uplifting and positive music.

Notes:

"For we walk by faith, not by sight." (2 Corinthians 5:7)

Activity 6: Set Your House in Order

"Look at the birds of the air: they neither sow nor reap nor gather into barns, and yet your heavenly Father feeds them. Are you not of more value than they?" (Matthew 6:26)

As the saying goes, "A cluttered desk is the sign of a cluttered mind." The same can be said for our homes. Clutter is not only inefficient, but it's also stressful, causes underlying anxiety that saps our precious energy, and—most importantly—distracts us from being in harmony and focused on God. This month's activity is to remove as much clutter as possible and set your house in order.

Are you already feeling anxiety? Don't worry, change is hard, and anxiety is normal when change is near. It will pass. Here's what I did. I went room by room and identified items I didn't need. I then sold them for a little extra pocket cash or found someone who needed them and gave them away. Once I had thinned the herd, I felt like a huge weight had been lifted and realized I don't need a bunch of stuff to be fulfilled.

Scripture Reading

Read Colossians Chapter 3, verses 1 through 17. Take note of anything that "jumps out at you" and pray to God to help you understand it and actualize it in your life.

Helpers

- Go room by room, cupboard by cupboard, closet by closet, and label things you haven't used in 6 months and don't need.
- If you get too stressed or anxious, take a walk and talk to God about it. Pray to Him for courage to face your fear of change and ask Him for strength to conquer it.

Notes:

"I pray that your faith might not rest in the wisdom of men but in the ***power*** *of God." (1 Corinthians 2:5)*

Activity 7: Use Social Media to Glorify God

"God comforts us in all our affliction, so that we may be able to comfort those who are in any affliction, with the comfort with which we ourselves are comforted by God." (2 Corinthians 1:4)

"Oh give thanks to the Lord; call upon his name; make known his deeds among the peoples! Sing to him, sing praises to him; tell of all his wondrous works!" (Psalm 105)

This month's activity is to use your social media platforms to glorify God. First, testify how God has helped you through your activities in life, how you trust him, and how you know He will help you through all your current and future activities. Next, share every miracle you witness and any scriptures that speak to your heart. Then, share encouraging scriptures about God's power and hope with those who are struggling.

Scripture Reading

Read Hebrews 10:19-39 and Colossians 3:1-17. Journal anything that speaks to your heart and ask God to help you understand it and apply it to your life.

Helpers

- Post memes with beautiful images of God's scriptures.
- Testify with a spirit of tenderness and love for God and your friends and family.

Notes:

The apostles said to the Lord, "Increase our faith!" (Luke 17:5)

If you are lacking faith, cry out to the Lord and ask Him to increase your faith. He will.

Activity 8: Sing Praises to God

"Sing praises to God, sing praises; sing praises to our King, sing praises." (Psalms 47:6)

"Praise the Lord. Praise the Lord, my soul. I will praise the Lord all my life; I will sing praise to my God as long as I live." (Psalm 146)

Sing like The Lord is listening… because He is. I have never met anybody who doesn't love to sing, but I have met many people who criticize their own voice so they don't end up singing as much as they should. Singing is good for our souls, and when we sing songs of praise to the Lord, it pleases Him greatly.

For the next 30 days, sing along with a worship song at least once per day like nobody but God is listening. Don't judge your voice; God thinks your voice is beautiful.

Scripture Reading

Read Psalms 145 through Psalm 150. Mediate on these scriptures daily throughout the month and pray them out loud to God.

Helpers

- Make a playlist of worship songs to sing along with during the month.

- Make up songs as you read the Psalms.
- Sing to the Lord no matter where you are, even if you just sing "Thank you for my blessings Lord, you are a great God, and you are the apple of my eye."

Notes:

"God will supply ***every need*** *of yours according to his riches in glory in Christ Jesus." (Philippians 4:19)*

Do you believe this yet?

Activity 9: Make Time to Rest

"Come to me, all who labor and are heavy laden, and I will give you rest." (Matthew 11:28)

I don't know about you, but sometimes I fall into the trap of trying to please everyone and find it hard to say no. The world says that in order to be a good woman, wife, and/or mom we must say yes to everything and everyone. The problem is, when we do this, we neglect ourselves, get run down, get sick or burned out, and end up being no good to anyone. This month it's time to rest and *make* time for your health and wellness.

You need rest and reinvigoration. God did not design you to go, go, go constantly. Even Jesus often took long rests in the desert away from everyone to hear the counsel of angels. This activity is all about taking care of yourself so you can be in the best state of wellness to serve the Lord and others with a glad heart.

Every day for the next 30 days make a little time for yourself to rest. This month give yourself permission to say no when you are feeling overwhelmed. Spend more time in God's rest and you will be greatly reinvigorated.

Scripture Reading

Read the Gospel of Matthew, Chapter 11 and Psalm 23. Write down verses that speak to you and ask God to help you understand them and actualize them in your daily life and relationships.

Helpers

- Meditate.
- Take a walk.
- Read a book.
- Take a bath.
- Meditate in silence, focusing on a scripture you love.
- Thoroughly rest on all Sundays.
- Seek peace.

Notes:

"Be still and know that I am God." (Psalm 46:10)

Activity 10: Appreciate God's Beauty

"Charm is deceitful, and beauty is vain, but a woman who fears the Lord is to be praised." (Proverbs 31:30)

"I praise you, for I am fearfully and wonderfully made. Wonderful are your works; my soul knows it very well." (Psalm 139:14)

This month I'm challenging you to fill your camera lens with at least one lovely image per day—starting with a beautiful portrait of someone you love dearly.

God commands us to: "Fix your eyes on whatever is lovely and praiseworthy." (Philippians 4:8). Also, lovely things bring peace to our minds and get our thoughts and affections focused on God's goodness rather than our fears and anxieties.

And remember, Jesus, God's word made flesh, is the most beautiful entity in the entire universe because He is the fullness of God's love for us. So take photos of anything that remind you of Jesus and His healing power and share with those who need reminders of His power.

Scripture Reading

Read Philippians 2:1-18. Note any words or verses that stick out and pray about them with God. Share an encouraging verse with a friend.

Helpers

- Make creative pictures or photos of Scriptures that speak to your spirit.
- Take pictures of trees, food, flowers, ponds, pets, birds, squirrels, someone you love, sun flare, sunset, stars, reflection, shadow, food—anything that is lovely and praiseworthy that glorifies God's creative genius.
- Create an album on your smart phone and at the end of the month create a slideshow or even have a small photo book printed. You can then look back as often as you want and be reminded of all God's glory around you.

Notes:

"Behold, I am the LORD, the God of all flesh. Is anything too hard for me?" (Jeremiah 32:27)

Activity 11: List your Blessings

"Every good gift and every perfect gift is from above, coming down from the Father of lights with whom there is no variation or shadow due to change." (James 1:17)

"Rejoice in the Lord always; again I will say, rejoice… do not be anxious about anything, but in everything by prayer and supplication with thanksgiving let your requests be made known to God. And the peace of God, which surpasses all understanding, will guard your hearts and your minds in Christ Jesus." (Philippians 4:4)

It's so easy to get distracted from our blessings and focus on what might feel like unfairness in our lives. I've learned one of the most effective ways for eliminating this and other anxieties is to count my blessings by listing them out. Every time I do this God humbles me and reminds me of how truly blessed I am. For the next 30 days, every time you feel stress or anxiety, list your blessings.

Scripture Reading

Read 1 Thessalonians 5:16-19 and Psalm 107. Consider each story in Psalm 107 and how they mirror your own life trials. Recognize how God has also delivered you from your troubles and give Him thanks and praise for every time He has rescued you.

Helpers

- List one blessing a day, and at the end of the activity you will have 30 blessings you can always reflect on and add to.
- Instead of focusing on big blessings, think of small ones, starting with the fact that you can breathe on your own, walk, talk, and think with a sound mind.
- Thank God for every possible "good" thing you can think of (especially all the people in your life who love you and encourage you), remembering that "every good and perfect gift comes down from heaven," (James 1:17)

Notes:

"For everyone who has been born of God overcomes the world. And this is the victory that has overcome the world: our faith." (1 John 5:4)

Activity 12: Pray Without Ceasing

"Therefore I tell you, whatever you ask for in prayer, believe that you have received it, and it will be yours." (Mark 11:24)

"Fear not, for I am with you; be not dismayed, for I am your God; I will strengthen you, I will help you, I will uphold you with my righteous right hand." Isaiah 41:10

"Pray without ceasing." (1 Thessalonians 5:17)

As I testified in our book "The Last Breakup" (available on Amazon), my spiritual journey started with a prayer for God's help. Prayer is also how I have conquered every obstacle since the day I decided to follow Jesus. When I made prayer a daily priority, I witnessed multiple miracles in my life and the lives of my children and others I prayed for. In fact, my life changed for the better in every way and I grew much closer to God. The power of prayer is truly amazing.

For the next 30 days, pray a minimum of three times per day. When you pray, pray with gratitude and belief, and remember God's way is always the best way.

Scripture Reading:

Read Psalm 91, Psalm 139:1-18, Psalm 23, and Psalm 27.

Helpers

Use the five finger prayer guide:

- Thumb: prayer for others—especially those closest to you and fellow believers.
- Index: Pray for teachers and servants (including all public servants, police, medical, first responders of all kinds, military, etc)
- Middle: Pray for leaders (including parents and guardians of all kinds).
- Ring: Pray for the weak (especially the sick and weak of faith).
- Little: Pray for yourself
- Pray for faith. Faith comes from God.

Notes:

"For everyone who has been born of God overcomes the world. And this is the victory that has overcome the world—our ***faith****." (1 John 5:4)*

Conclusion

I hope and pray this devotional book has been a great blessing for you and that the good habits you've developed become a part of your every day life. I pray you continue to put all your faith and hope in God and that your relationship with Him continues to grow. I pray you continue to seek new activities to grow closer to God through Christ our Redeemer, fully trusting this beautiful promise:

> *"But those who hope in the LORD will renew their strength. They will soar on wings like eagles; they will run and not grow weary, they will walk and not be faint." (Isaiah 40:31)*

If you need to contact me, please email me or request speaking engagement, prayer, or anything else, send an email to: breakthroughvictory@gmail.com

And remember:

"All things are possible for those who believe." (Mark 9:23)

Prayers

Sometimes it's hard to know how to pray or what to pray for. You can always start with the Lord's Prayer. When we pray from our heart it seems easier. Here are some prayers to help you out if needed.

The Lord's Prayer

Our Father who art in heaven, hallowed be Thy name. Thy kingdom come. Thy will be done in earth as it is in heaven. Give us this day our daily bread. Forgive us our trespasses as we forgive those who trespass against us. Lead us not into temptation but deliver us from evil. For thine is the Kingdom, the Power and the Glory forever. Amen." (Matthew 6: 9–13)

Praise and Thankfulness

When you start your prayer in Praise you are approaching God with respect and honor.

Yours, O LORD, is the greatness, the power, the glory, the victory, and the majesty. Everything in the heavens and on earth is yours, O LORD, and this is your kingdom. We adore you as the one who is over all things." (1 Chronicles 29:11)

Repentance

When you **repent**, you are asking **God** for forgiveness, then you must turn away from the sin.

"If I had not confessed the sin in my heart, my Lord would not have listened." (Psalm 66:18)

Ask

God wants us to ask Him for our needs in prayer. Just make sure its your needs and not your greeds.

"Don't worry about anything, instead pray about everything. Tell God what you need and thank him for all he has done!" (Philippians 4:6)

Yield

Prayer is all about recognizing that God is in complete control. We need to remember that our will is not always allied with Gods will.

"Father...not my will, but yours be done" (Luke 22:42)

Summarize Your Learnings

Summarize your learnings from the past year and state your goals for the next year.

Scripture About Faith

Hebrews 11 (© New International Version)

Faith in Action

Now faith is confidence in what we hope for and
assurance about what we do not see. [2] This is what
the ancients were commended for.

By faith we understand that the universe was formed at God's command, so that what is seen was not made out of what was visible.

By faith Abel brought God a better offering than Cain did. By faith he was commended as righteous, when God spoke well of his offerings. And by faith Abel still speaks, even though he is dead.

By faith Enoch was taken from this life, so that he did
not experience death: "He could not be found,
because God had taken him away." For before he was
taken, he was commended as one who pleased
God. [6] And without faith it is impossible to please
God, because anyone who comes to him must believe
that he exists and that he rewards those who
earnestly seek him.

By faith Noah, when warned about things not yet seen, in holy fear built an ark to save his family. By his faith he condemned the world and became heir of the righteousness that is in keeping with faith.

By faith Abraham, when called to go to a place he would later receive as his inheritance, obeyed and went, even though he did not know where he was going. By faith he made his home in the promised land like a stranger in a foreign country; he lived in tents, as did Isaac and Jacob, who were heirs with him of the same promise. For he was looking forward to the city with foundations, whose architect and builder is God. And by faith even Sarah, who was past childbearing age, was enabled to bear children because she considered him faithful who had made the promise. And so from this one man, and he as good as dead, came descendants as numerous as the stars in the sky and as countless as the sand on the seashore.

All these people were still living by faith when they died. They did not receive the things promised; they only saw them and welcomed them from a distance, admitting that they were foreigners and strangers on earth. People who say such things show that they are looking for a country of their own. If they had been thinking of the country they had left, they would have had opportunity to return. [16] Instead, they were longing for a better country—a heavenly one. Therefore God is not ashamed to be called their God, for he has prepared a city for them.

By faith Abraham, when God tested him, offered Isaac as a sacrifice. He who had embraced the promises was about to sacrifice his one and only son, even though God had said to him, "It is through Isaac that your offspring will be reckoned." Abraham reasoned that God could even raise the dead, and so in a manner of speaking he did receive Isaac back from death.

By faith Isaac blessed Jacob and Esau in regard to their future.

By faith Jacob, when he was dying, blessed each of Joseph's sons, and worshiped as he leaned on the top of his staff.

By faith Joseph, when his end was near, spoke about the exodus of the Israelites from Egypt and gave instructions concerning the burial of his bones.

By faith Moses' parents hid him for three months after he was born, because they saw he was no ordinary child, and they were not afraid of the king's edict.

By faith Moses, when he had grown up, refused to be known as the son of Pharaoh's daughter. He chose to be mistreated along with the people of God rather than to enjoy the fleeting pleasures of sin. He regarded disgrace for the sake of Christ as of greater value than the treasures of Egypt, because he was looking ahead to his reward. By faith he left Egypt, not fearing the king's anger; he persevered because he saw him who is invisible. By faith he kept the Passover and the application of blood, so that the destroyer of the firstborn would not touch the firstborn of Israel.

By faith the people passed through the Red Sea as on dry land; but when the Egyptians tried to do so, they were drowned.

By faith the walls of Jericho fell, after the army had marched around them for seven days.

By faith the prostitute Rahab, because she welcomed the spies, was not killed with those who were disobedient.

And what more shall I say? I do not have time to tell about Gideon, Barak,Samson and Jephthah, about David and Samuel and the prophets, who through faith conquered kingdoms, administered justice, and gained what was promised; who shut the mouths of lions, quenched the fury of the flames, and escaped the edge of the sword; whose weakness was turned to strength; and who became powerful in battle and routed foreign armies. Women received back their dead, raised to life again. There were others who were tortured, refusing to be released so that they might gain an even better resurrection. Some faced jeers and flogging, and even chains and imprisonment. They were put to death by stoning; they were sawed in two; they were killed by the sword. They went about in sheepskins and goatskins, destitute, persecuted and mistreated— the world was not worthy of them. They wandered in deserts and mountains, living in caves and in holes in the ground.

These were all commended for their faith…"

And rest assured, you too will be commended for YOUR faith!

Mark 9:14-29 (© New International Version)

"When they came to the other disciples, they saw a large crowd around them and the teachers of the law arguing with them.15 As soon as all the people saw Jesus, they were overwhelmed with wonder and ran to greet him.

"What are you arguing with them about?" he asked.

A man in the crowd answered, "Teacher, I brought you my son, who is possessed by a spirit that has robbed him of speech. Whenever it seizes him, it throws him to the ground. He foams at the mouth, gnashes his teeth and becomes rigid. I asked your disciples to drive out the spirit, but they could not.

"You unbelieving generation," Jesus replied, "how long shall I stay with you? How long shall I put up with you? Bring the boy to me."

So they brought him. When the spirit saw Jesus, it immediately threw the boy into a convulsion. He fell to the ground and rolled around, foaming at the mouth.

Jesus asked the boy's father, "How long has he been like this?"

"From childhood," he answered. "It has often thrown him into fire or water to kill him. But if you can do anything, take pity on us and help us."

"'If you can'?" said Jesus. **"All things are possible for those who believe."**

Immediately the boy's father exclaimed, "I do believe; help me overcome my unbelief!"

When Jesus saw that a crowd was running to the scene, he rebuked the impure spirit. "You deaf and mute spirit," he said, "I command you, come out of him and never enter him again."

The spirit shrieked, convulsed him violently and came out. The boy looked so much like a corpse that many said, "He's dead." But Jesus took him by the hand and lifted him to his feet, and he stood up.

After Jesus had gone indoors, his disciples asked him privately, "Why couldn't we drive it out?"

He replied, "This kind can come out only by prayer."

Now the question is: do you believe? Notice how the man asked Jesus to HELP Him overcome his unbelief, which is his weak faith. So, remember: if you need more faith to overcome an obstacle, confess your weakness to God and ask Him to HELP you have more faith!

"Lord, increase our faith!" -the apostles to Jesus in Luke 17.

Mark 11:22

And Jesus answered them, "Have faith in God. Truly, I say to you, whoever says to this mountain, 'Be taken up and thrown into the sea,' and does not doubt in his heart, but believes that what he says will come to pass, it will be done for him. Therefore I tell you, whatever you ask in prayer, believe that you have received it…"

Do you believe in the power of faith? If not, start talking to more Christians and ask them to testify to you. The Bible says "They overcame (and got more faith) by the blood of the lamb and word of their testimonies." (Rev. 12:11)

Psalm 23

A Psalm of David. The Lord is my shepherd; I shall not want. He makes me lie down in green pastures. He leads me beside still waters. He restores my soul. He leads me in paths of righteousness for his name's sake. Even though I walk through the valley of the shadow of death, I will fear no evil, for you are with me; your rod and your staff, they comfort me. You prepare a table before me in the presence of my enemies; you anoint my head with oil; my cup overflows.

Psalm 27

The Lord is my light and my salvation—
whom shall I fear?
The Lord is the stronghold of my life—
of whom shall I be afraid?
2 When the wicked advance against me
to devour[a] me,
it is my enemies and my foes
who will stumble and fall.
3 Though an army besiege me,
my heart will not fear;
though war break out against me,
even then I will be confident.
4 One thing I ask from the Lord,
this only do I seek:
that I may dwell in the house of the Lord
all the days of my life,
to gaze on the beauty of the Lord
and to seek him in his temple.
5 For in the day of trouble
he will keep me safe in his dwelling;
he will hide me in the shelter of his sacred tent
and set me high upon a rock.
6 Then my head will be exalted
above the enemies who surround me;
at his sacred tent I will sacrifice with shouts of joy;
I will sing and make music to the Lord.

7 Hear my voice when I call, Lord;
be merciful to me and answer me.
8 My heart says of you, "Seek his face!"
Your face, Lord, I will seek.
9 Do not hide your face from me,
do not turn your servant away in anger;
you have been my helper.
Do not reject me or forsake me,
God my Savior.
10 Though my father and mother forsake me,
the Lord will receive me.
11 Teach me your way, Lord;
lead me in a straight path
because of my oppressors.
12 Do not turn me over to the desire of my foes,
for false witnesses rise up against me,
spouting malicious accusations.
13 I remain confident of this:
I will see the goodness of the Lord
in the land of the living.
14 Wait for the Lord;
be strong and take heart
and wait for the Lord.

"For God so loved the world, that he gave his only Son, that whoever believes in him should not perish but have eternal life. For God did not send his Son into the world to condemn the world, but in order that the world might be saved through him." (John 3:16-17)

Faith Journal

www.ingramcontent.com/pod-product-compliance
Lightning Source LLC
LaVergne TN
LVHW010628100826
845148LV00014B/3163

* 9 7 8 0 9 6 6 3 9 1 7 3 2 *